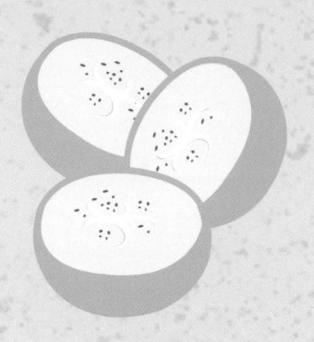

eat smart

Vegetables

Vic Parker

Quarto
Knows

Quarto is the authority on a wide range of topics.

Quarto educates, entertains and enriches the lives of our readers—enthusiasts and lovers of hands-on living.

www.quartoknows.com

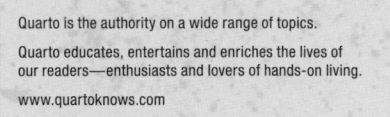

Ask an adult for help

Always ask an adult to help you make the recipes and get all the ingredients and equipment ready. Remember to wash your hands before you start.

First published in hardback in the UK in 2017 by
QED Publishing
Part of The Quarto Group
The Old Brewery, 6 Blundell Street,
London, N7 9BH

A catalogue record for this book is available from the British Library.

ISBN 978 1 78493 721 8

Printed and bound in China

Publisher: Maxime Boucknooghe
Editorial Director: Victoria Garrard
Art Director: Miranda Snow
Design and Editorial: Starry Dog Books Ltd
Consultant: Charlotte Stirling-Reed BSc (hons), MSc, RNutr (Public Health)

Picture credits
(t=top, b=bottom, l=left, r=right, c=centre, fc=front cover)

Alamy 12cl Agripicture Images/Peter Dean, 13bl Itani, 14cl David Chilvers, 14cr Mark Saunders, 15tl Cultura/Bill Sykes, 20cl Nigel Cattlin

Corbis 4bl (lettuce) Fancy/Veer

FLPA 21tr Nigel Cattlin

Getty Images 15br Iconica/Andersen Ross

Photolibrary 9br Fresh Food Images/Tim Hill, 12br Chris L Jones, 13tr Botanica, 15cr Johner/Anna Skoog, 21cl (King Edward) Foodpix/Gottlieb Dennis, 21b Foodpix/Ann Stratton

Shutterstock fc Elena Schweitzer, fc mashe, fc Andrjuss, fc Norma Cornes, fc Filipe B. Varela, fc science photo, fc khz, fc Andrjuss, fc Sandra Caldwell, fc AlenKadr, fc artcasta, fc Evgeny Karandaev, fc Debu55y, 4cl Egor Rodynchenko, 4cr Tim UR, 4bl Matt Mohd, 4bc Mashe, 4br Yellowj, 5tl WitR, 5tr Simon Booth, 5b (soil) Elnur, 5bl Elena Schweitzer, 5bc (leek) S.Fierros, 5br (onion) Norma Cornes, 5br (beetroot) Filipe B. Varela, 6c Lepas, 6bc Binh Thanh Bui, 7tl Mashe, 7tr Sergey Kolodkin, 7cr Yellowj, 7bl Harris Shiffman, 7br Andrjuss, 8tl Joe Gough, 8cl Alena Ozerova, 8r Thomas M Perkins, 8bl Khz, 9cl martinlee, 11tl Sandra Caldwell,11tr (carrots) Mashe, 11cl Yellowj, 11bl Paul Cowan, 11br (beetroot) Sergey Kolodkin, 11br (broccoli) Andrjuss, 11br (half courgette) PhotoPips, 11br (pepper) Paul Cowan, 12tr Yellowj, 13cl Leonid Shcheglov, 13br (pea)?, 14tr Mashe, 14bl Christopher Halloran, 15bl Volosina, 17bl PhotoPips, 17br Sandra Caldwell, 20tr Andrjuss, 20cr Rafa Fabrykiewicz, 20br Oxana Zuboff, 21cl Angela Hawkey

Public domain 11br (corns)

Words in **bold** are explained in the glossary on page 22.

Contents

Vegetables

Vegetables are parts of plants that we usually eat as savoury foods.

Cauliflower

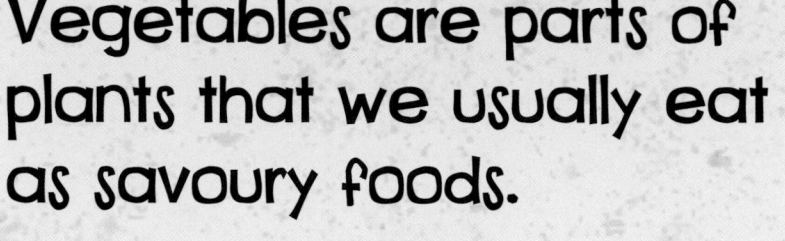

There are many different types of vegetable, such as cauliflower, celery, peas, carrots and courgettes.

Celery

Courgettes

Peas

Carrots

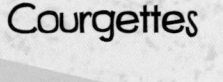

You will need:

- An empty eggshell
- Some cotton wool
- Egg cup
- Felt-tip pens
- Water
- Cress seeds

Grow a cress plant

1 Take the large half of an empty eggshell and fill it with cotton wool.

2 Put your shell in an egg cup and draw a funny face on it with felt-tip pens.

3 Pour some water onto the cotton wool to make it very wet. Then sprinkle some cress seeds onto the cotton wool.

4 Water the seeds every day and wait for the egg's cress 'hair' to sprout. Sprinkle your cress onto sandwiches or salads.

Sometimes we eat the leaves of vegetable plants, such as lettuces and cabbages. We also eat the stems of plants such as leeks.

Some vegetables, such as onions and beetroot, have tasty parts that grow underground.

Cabbage   Lettuce   Leek   Onion   Beetroot

Vegetables around the world

Different types of vegetables are grown around the world.

Vegetables need the right conditions in order to grow. Some need hot, dry weather. Others prefer plenty of rain.

North America

South America

Courgettes are grown in warm parts of North America.

Cassava is a **root vegetable** that grows well in the tropical parts of South America.

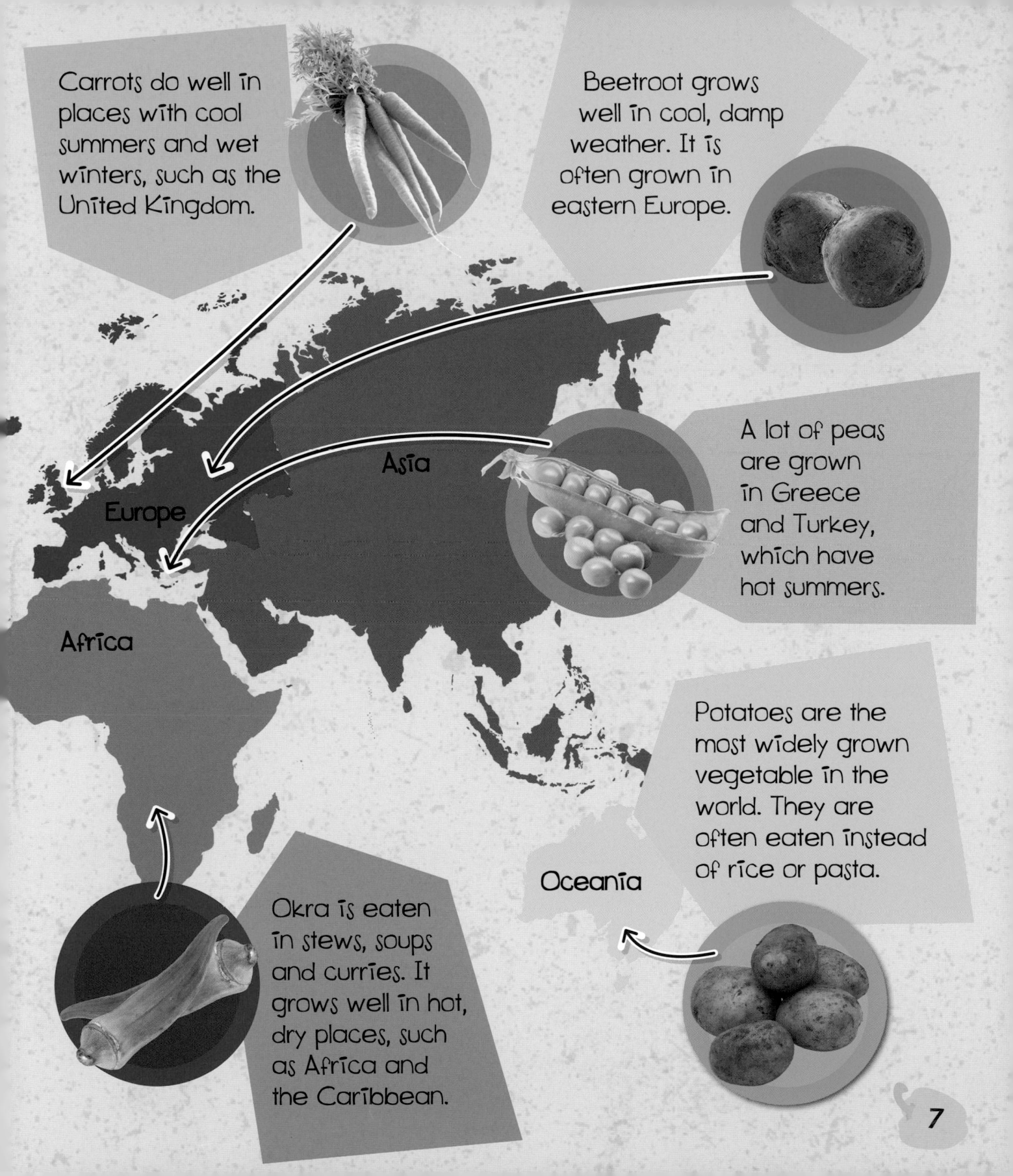

Carrots do well in places with cool summers and wet winters, such as the United Kingdom.

Beetroot grows well in cool, damp weather. It is often grown in eastern Europe.

A lot of peas are grown in Greece and Turkey, which have hot summers.

Asia

Europe

Africa

Potatoes are the most widely grown vegetable in the world. They are often eaten instead of rice or pasta.

Oceania

Okra is eaten in stews, soups and curries. It grows well in hot, dry places, such as Africa and the Caribbean.

Vegetables in meals

Vegetables give us a huge range of flavours in the food we eat each day.

For breakfast, we might have a spinach or sweet potato omelette.

For lunch, we might have a bowl of vegetable soup or a salad.

For dinner, we might eat a Chinese vegetable stir fry.

8

Ingredients:

- Half a butternut squash
- Half a red pepper
- 6 mange-tout
- 1 small carrot
- A few slices of aubergine
- 1 small stick of celery
- 2 or 4 mushrooms
- 1 tsp olive oil
- 2 wholemeal pittas
- 2 tbsp hummus

Makes: 2 servings

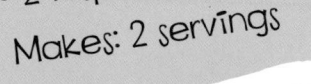

Make a vegetable pitta

1 Peel and chop the butternut squash. Ask an adult to boil it for about 15 minutes.

2 Ask an adult to help you slice the other vegetables.

3 Ask an adult to help you heat the olive oil in a frying pan for one minute. Add the butternut squash and other vegetables, and lightly fry them until they go soft.

4 Warm the pittas under the grill, then slice them open and spread some hummus inside. Fill with the vegetables and serve.

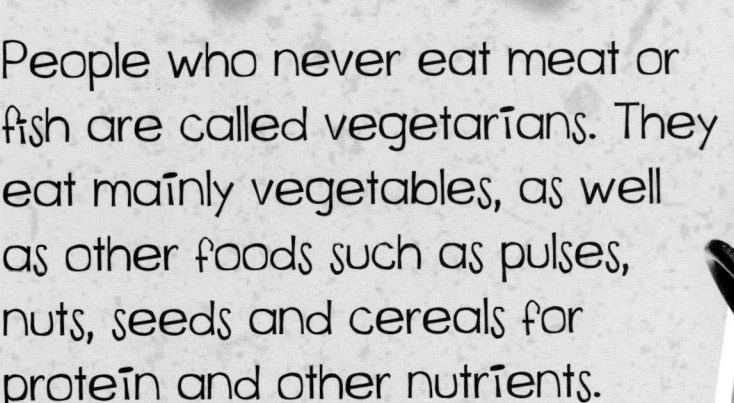

People who never eat meat or fish are called vegetarians. They eat mainly vegetables, as well as other foods such as pulses, nuts, seeds and cereals for protein and other nutrients.

This Indian dish combines spices and lots of vegetables, such as cauliflower.

9

Vegetables for a healthy body

Vegetables are packed with vitamins and minerals that are good for our bodies.

Vegetables such as cauliflower contain **fibre**, which helps to keep our **digestive systems** healthy.

Vegetables such as broccoli contain iron. Iron helps to make red blood cells, which carry oxygen around our bodies.

Carrots contain vitamin C, which helps our bodies to **absorb** iron from food. It also helps our bodies to heal.

Red pepper

Red peppers contain vitamin C, which helps our bodies to fight off illness.

As well as vitamin C, carrots also contain vitamin A, which is good for eyesight.

Carrots

Peas

Peas are high in fibre. They also contain vitamin K, which helps wounds to heal properly.

Food fact
To stay healthy, we should eat at least five portions of different vegetables and fruits a day.

1

2

3

4

5

Growing peas

Peas grow best in soil that has had **compost** dug into it. The compost adds nutrients to the soil.

Peas

1 Pea seeds can be sown or planted in the ground in spring and early summer. The seedlings need lots of water to grow well.

After about nine weeks, flowers appear. The seeds inside the flowers swell and turn into peas, which grow inside **pods**.

2

Pea pods are heavy, so the farmer puts up wire or netting to support the plants. Long, thin **tendrils** on the plants coil around the wire and hold the plants up.

3

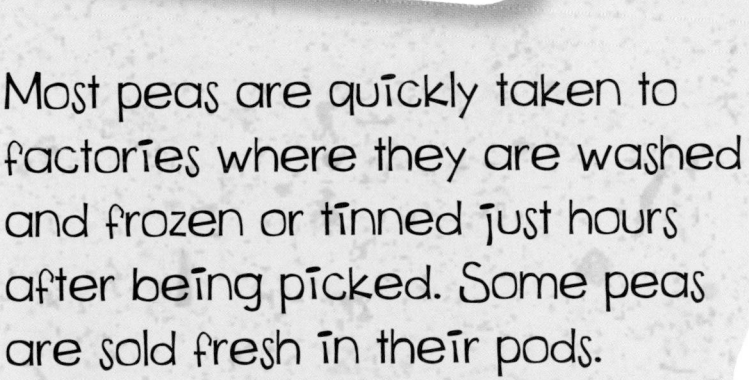

4

After three weeks, the peas are ready to **harvest**. Special machines pull up the plants and remove the peas from their pods.

Most peas are quickly taken to factories where they are washed and frozen or tinned just hours after being picked. Some peas are sold fresh in their pods.

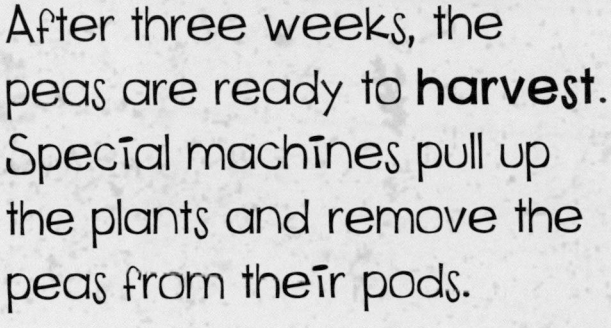

Food fact

Peas eaten straight from the pod are super-sweet and tasty. Try some and see!

5

13

Growing carrots

Carrots grow well in soil that has been weeded.

Carrots

1 Carrot seeds can be sown or planted any time from early spring to mid summer.

Seedlings start to appear 15 to 20 days after planting.

3 The carrots we eat are the roots of the plants. They grow under the soil, so you can't see them in a carrot field.

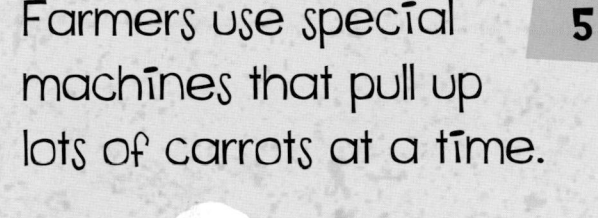

When the leafy tops start to wilt, the vegetables are ready to harvest. This may be any time from mid summer to early autumn.

4

Farmers use special machines that pull up lots of carrots at a time.

5

Many carrots are taken to shops and sold fresh. Some are tinned or frozen.

6

Food fact

Just one medium carrot counts as one serving of your five-a-day veggies.

Grow some courgettes

Courgettes are easy to grow. One plant will give you lots of courgettes.

In the spring, fill a small pot with compost. Plant a seed about two centimetres deep, on its edge – this will help to stop it rotting. Water it and put it indoors in a sunny place.

1

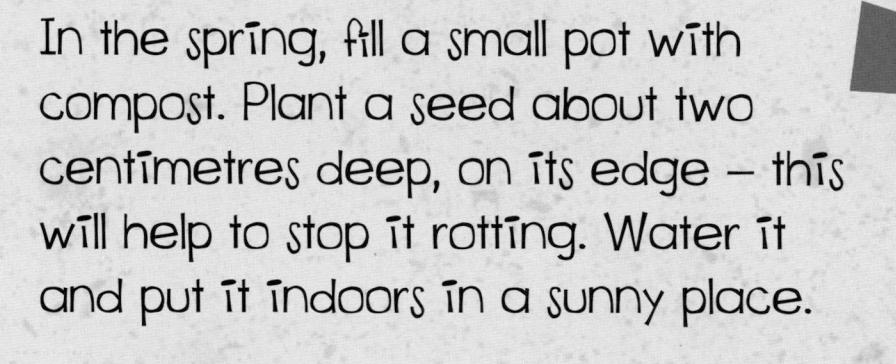

2

When roots start to push through the hole in the bottom of the pot, move the plant to a medium-sized pot. Water it and put it outdoors if the weather is warm.

3 After two months, carefully tip your courgette plant out of its pot and replant it in a bucket.

Courgette plants produce large, yellow flowers. The courgettes grow behind some of the flowers. They are ready to pick when they are about 10 centimetres long.

4

Food fact

Did you know you can eat courgette flowers? First wash the flowers, then chop them into a salad or add them to a pasta dish.

Make courgette boats

Have fun making these tasty little courgette boats.

Ingredients:

- 2 large courgettes
- 1 onion, finely chopped
- 2 garlic cloves, finely chopped
- 4 tsp vegetable oil
- 3 small mushrooms, chopped
- 6 tomatoes, finely chopped
- Black pepper
- 2 tbsp of breadcrumbs
- 2 tbsp of Parmesan cheese, grated

Makes: 4 servings

1 Ask an adult to set the oven to 180°C/350°F/Gas 6. Cut the courgettes in half. Scoop out the insides and put them to one side.

2 Ask an adult to lightly fry the onions and garlic in oil until they begin to soften.

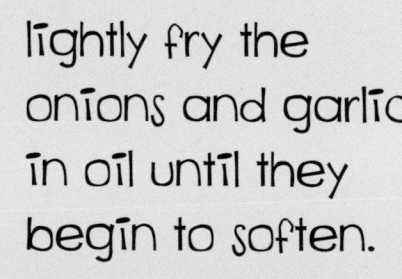

3 Add the insides of the courgettes, the mushrooms, tomatoes and a little black pepper. Fry for five minutes.

Mix the breadcrumbs and grated cheese together in a bowl.

4

5 Put the courgette boats on a baking tray. Fill each one with fried vegetables, then sprinkle on the breadcrumb and cheese topping.

Ask an adult to put them in the oven and cook them for 30 minutes. Serve straight away.

6

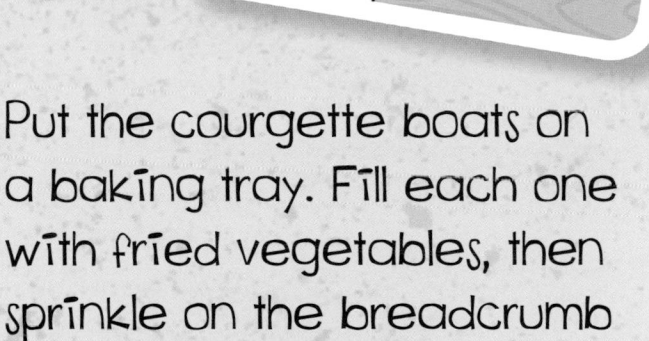

Growing potatoes

Potatoes

Potatoes grow best in cool climates.

Old potatoes produce buds, or 'eyes'. If they are planted in spring, the buds grow into young potato plants.

The plants produce new potatoes, which grow under the soil.

When the leaves of the plants turn yellow, the farmer starts to harvest the crop. Harvesting is done from early summer to late autumn.

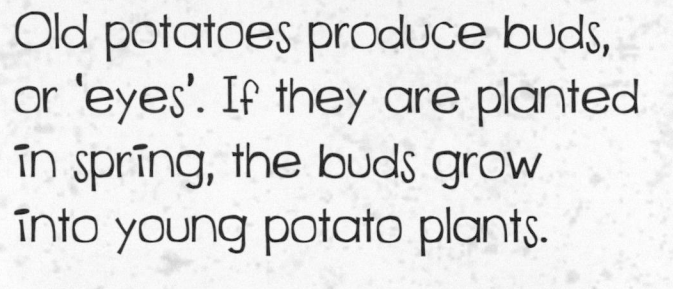

Each plant produces several potatoes. Farmers use a special machine to pull the potatoes from the ground.

4

5

Most potatoes are taken to shops to be sold fresh. Some go to factories, where they are turned into foods such as frozen chips or crisps.

King Edward

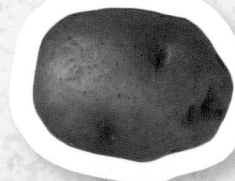

Desirée

Food fact

There are thousands of potato varieties. These are just a few of them! But remember, potatoes do not count as one of your five-a-day vegetables because they are too **starchy**.

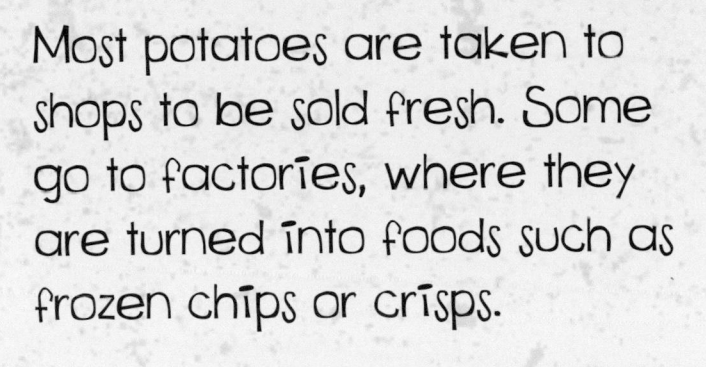

Maris Piper

Rooster

Glossary

Absorb
To take something in.

Compost
Rotting plant material added to soil to improve its quality.

Digestive system
All the parts of our body that are involved in breaking down and using food, and getting rid of waste products.

Fibre
Fibre is the part of plants that our bodies cannot digest. There are two types of fibre – insoluble and soluble. Both types are important for a healthy, balanced diet. Insoluble fibre makes it easier for our bodies to get rid of waste food. Soluble fibre helps to keep our digestive system healthy.

Harvest
To gather, or collect, crops from the field.

Pods
The long, flat parts of a pea plant that contain the peas.

Root vegetable
The enlarged root of a plant that we eat as a vegetable.

Starchy
Containing starch – a white, tasteless carbohydrate found in foods such as potatoes, rice and wheat flour.

Tendrils
Thin coiling parts of plants that help support the stem by coiling around or clinging to objects.

Index

Next steps

* Show the children a variety of vegetables. Discuss their size, shape, colour and texture.

* Find photographs of what different vegetables look like when they are growing. Choose one to draw and then label the different parts of the plant (roots, stem, branches and leaves).

* Discuss which vegetables we can eat raw and which we need to cook. Talk about which parts we can eat and which parts we should throw away.

* Discuss why our bodies need vegetables to stay healthy. Talk about why it is important to eat five portions a day, and why it's best to eat different kinds of vegetables.

* Talk about which local vegetables are available in different seasons.

* Ask the children to keep a vegetable diary for a week to see how many vegetables, and which types, they eat each day. Suggest ways they could include vegetables in their meals and snacks.

* Explain the conditions each vegetable needs to grow and talk about where each vegetable grows in the world. Look at a map or globe to identify the places where each vegetable comes from.

* Collect the packaging from various vegetables bought in shops. On a map, mark the countries where they came from. Make an international vegetable cookbook with recipes and pictures from around the world.